SPOTLIGHT ON NATIVE AMERICANS

OJIBWE

Torren Ramsey

PowerKiDS
press.

New York

Published in 2016 by The Rosen Publishing Group, Inc.
29 East 21st Street, New York, NY 10010

First Edition

Editor: Karolena Bielecki
Book Design: Kris Everson
Reviewed by: Robert J. Conley, Former Sequoyah Distinguished Professor at Western Carolina University and Director of Native American Studies at Morningside College and Montana State University
Supplemental material reviewed by: Donald A. Grinde, Jr., Professor of Transnational/American Studies at the State University of New York at Buffalo.

Photo Credits: Cover © Thomas Sbampato/imageBroker/age fotostock; pp. 4–5 CalamityJohn2/Pond5.com; p. 7 North Wind Picture Archives; p. 9 Underwood Archives\UIG/age fotostock; pp. 10, 19 Mille Lacs band (Minnesota); pp. 13, 17 Sun Valley/Nativestock Photography; pp. 14–15 AFP/Hulton Archive/Getty Images; pp. 20–21 © Interfoto/age fotostock; p. 23 Wikimedia/Hans-Jürgen Hübner; p. 24 Corbis/Ed Kashi; p. 27 David Cooper/Toronto Star/Getty Images; pp. 29–29 Joel Sartore/National Geographic Image Collection/Getty Images.

Library of Congress Cataloging-in-Publication Data

Ramsey, Torren.
  Ojibwe / Torren Ramsey.
    pages cm. — (Spotlight on Native Americans)
  Includes bibliographical references and index.
  ISBN 978-1-4994-1700-5 (pbk.)
  ISBN 978-1-4994-1701-2 (6 pack)
  ISBN 978-1-4994-1703-6 (library binding)
  1. Ojibwa Indians—History—Juvenile literature. 2. Ojibwa Indians—Government relations—Juvenile literature. 3. Ojibwa Indians—Social life and customs—Juvenile literature. I. Title.
  E99.C6R14 2016
  977.004'97333—dc23
                                    2015009238

Manufactured in the United States of America

CONTENTS

OJIBWE LAND AND ORIGINS

CHAPTER 1

One of the most numerous of the native populations in North America, the Ojibwes are scattered across the United States and Canada. The Ojibwe, Potawatomi, and Ottawa tribes were originally one people. Their traditional territory stretched from the northern Great Plains near present-day Lake Winnipeg in Manitoba, Canada, to the southeastern shores of the Great Lakes in today's United States, and from central Saskatchewan to southern Ontario in today's Canada.

No one knows exactly how the Ojibwes and other Native Americans came to North America. Like most native peoples, though, Ojibwes tell a traditional story to explain their origins. Long ago, only water covered the earth. Creator's helper, called Naanabozho, and his friends were floating on a raft. Naanabozho asked his friends to dive under the water and get some earth. Many tried and failed. Then Muskrat dived down and came back with sand in his paws. Naanabozho blew on the sand, spreading it over the water to create dry land. Muskrat kept diving for sand, and Naanabozho kept blowing on it until the land was large enough to support people.

The Ojibwes are also known as the Chippewas. However, they call themselves *Anishinaabe* or its plural, *Anishinaabeg*, which means "the people."

Many of the wilderness areas of the lakes and woods of Minnesota and Wisconsin have hardly changed since the time when the Ojibwes first met Europeans.

5

EARLY CONTACT WITH EUROPEANS

CHAPTER 2

Europeans came to North America beginning in the late fifteenth century in search of land, wealth, and religious freedom. The French began exploring the North American continent in the early 1600s looking for furs. Wanting to trade, they first came into contact with the Ojibwes in 1622. The traders and the Ojibwes soon built a strong **alliance** that benefited both peoples: the French got furs, while the Ojibwes received guns and other trade goods such as cast-iron pots, iron axes, and blankets. Guns helped the Ojibwes defend their territory.

The Ojibwes even kept out the powerful Haudenosaunees. The Europeans pushed the Haudenosaunees (called Iroquois by the Europeans) into the eastern side of the Ojibwes' territory in what is now Michigan.

In 1679, French trader Daniel du Luth persuaded Ojibwe leaders to attend a **council** with the Dakota-speaking people of the Seven Bands of the Teton. Du Luth helped these two traditional enemies form an alliance. Peace

Print of a French fur trader's camp. The Ojibwes were excellent hunters and trappers, and through their trade with the French, they became powerful and wealthy.

brought stability to the region, as well as more trade. The Ojibwes gained more hunting grounds to the west in Dakota-held territory in today's northern Minnesota and Wisconsin, while the Dakotas received a steadier supply of trade goods from the French.

WESTWARD MOVEMENT AND CONFLICT

CHAPTER 3

As the French fur trade moved westward, so did the Ojibwes. They spread out into the Great Lakes, the Great Plains, and what is now Michigan and Wisconsin in the United States and Ontario, Canada. The Ojibwe-Dakota alliance lasted until 1736, when the Dakotas broke. By 1750, the Ojibwes were occupying the land held by the Dakotas.

As more whites illegally moved onto natives' land, the Ojibwes battled the Dakotas and other neighboring tribes over the remaining hunting land from the mid-1700s to the mid-1800s. Fights such as the Battle of the Brulé in 1842 eventually resulted in Ojibwes permanently driving the Dakotas west across the Mississippi River. The Ojibwes sided with the French against the British during the French and Indian War (1754–1763), but the British prevailed and seized Canada from the French.

In 1776, the British and the Americans went to war over who would control the colonies in America. The

Americans, with the help of many **indigenous** nations, won the war and became the United States. The **Treaty** of Paris, signed at the end of the American Revolution (1783), established the boundaries between the United States and Canada, splitting the Ojibwes' territories between the two countries.

This colorized 1904 photograph shows Ojibwe hunters returning to their camp in Minnesota on a birch-bark canoe.

FORCED REMOVAL

CHAPTER 4

Through treaties, both the Americans and the British in Canada forced the Ojibwes to give up land. The U.S. and Canadian governments also wanted the Ojibwes to take up Euro-American-style farming and live in what the British called "model villages."

Tepee Interior

Life was hard for the Ojibwes during the nineteenth century as they were forced to give up more and more land to the U.S. and Canadian governments. This family was photographed in their home on a **reservation** in 1900.

These villages were designed to force the Ojibwes to assimilate, or to live like Euro-Americans and give up their tribal customs. By 1900, treaties had forced Ojibwes to move onto reservations. However, neither government stopped whites from illegally settling on Ojibwe land.

Ex-fur trader William Robinson **negotiated** a treaty between the Ojibwes living near Lake Superior and the Canadian government. In the treaty, the Ojibwes agreed to give the government some land. In return, the Canadians agreed that each Ojibwe band could select its own reservation site and each member of the bands would receive money for the land signed over to the government. The Canadians also promised that the Ojibwes would always be allowed to hunt and fish on those lands given to the government. This treaty was quickly broken. Ojibwes were kept from hunting and fishing on the lands. As nonnatives moved onto the reservations, they took more land from the Ojibwes, and the reservations shrank in size or disappeared.

RESERVATION LIFE
CHAPTER 5

The Canadian and U.S. governments broke their treaties with the Ojibwes. They allowed whites to settle illegally on the reservations. The settlers cut down timber, mined minerals, and destroyed the Ojibwes' rice fields and sugar maple trees. This made life hard for Ojibwes, who were used to living in an **environment** that provided plenty of food.

By the early 1900s, the Ojibwes were starving. Although part of both governments' plans included teaching Ojibwes European American farming methods, what little reservation land was left was often too poor to farm. Sometimes there was not even enough land to both live on and farm.

Canada and the United States passed laws forcing Ojibwes to send their children to **boarding schools**. Between the 1880s and 1940s, children as young as four were removed from their families. At school, children were punished for speaking their language. Boys spent summers working as laborers for white

Boys working in the blacksmith shop of an Indian boarding school. Many Ojibwe children were forced to leave their homes and families and go to boarding schools set up by the U.S. and Canadian governments.

farmers or factory owners, while girls worked as maids. They worked long hours and received little or no money for their labor. Many were not allowed to return home until they were eighteen. The Ojibwes, however, managed to hold on to their **culture**.

THE AMERICAN INDIAN MOVEMENT

CHAPTER 6

In the 1950s, the United States government moved families from reservations to large cities during the "Volunteer Relocation Program" so the government could claim more of the Ojibwes' land. The program was anything but voluntary. Many Ojibwes were actually forced to move to cities such as Minneapolis and St. Paul in Minnesota. By 1970, approximately half of the Ojibwes had been moved into urban centers.

The American Indian Movement (AIM) arose out of the government's pressure on these "urban Indians" to fully assimilate into white culture. Three Ojibwes— Dennis Banks, Clyde Bellecourt, and George Mitchell— founded AIM in Minneapolis in 1968. AIM's goal was to help Ojibwe children learn more about their own culture, language, and traditions.

The idea spread to other urban Native Americans interested in keeping their cultures alive. By 1971, AIM had become a national organization and included natives on reservations and in rural areas. AIM wanted to protect the traditions of all indigenous peoples. One way AIM and its supporters accomplished this was to bring legal cases to court to get the government to uphold indigenous treaty rights, such as the tribes' right to hunt, fish, and gather wild rice on their traditional lands.

In this photo from 1973, Federal troops block the road to Wounded Knee, South Dakota. Two hundred members of the AIM were petitioning the government for money to support the town, where hundreds of Lakota Sioux were killed in 1890.

TRADITIONAL OJIBWE LIFE

CHAPTER 7

For centuries, individual Ojibwe bands moved with the seasons. Over winter, they hunted and got furs ready for trading by scraping and **tanning** them. In spring, "sugar bush" camps reunited friends and families. Relatives gathered at the family's own section of maple forest. They tapped trees and collected sap in birch-bark containers, then boiled the sap down into syrup. Once this hardened, they put it in wooden troughs and pounded it into sugar. Each family processed 500 to 600 pounds (225 to 270 kg) of maple sugar annually.

In summer, villages north of Lakes Superior and Huron provided a base for fishing. Women made basswood-twine fishing nets. Men made deer-bone hooks for fishing with poles, and in winter, they used wooden, fish-shaped **decoys** to lure fish to holes cut in the ice. When the waters were clear of ice, they also spearfished at night by torchlight.

While men fished, women grew pumpkins, sweet potatoes, corn, beans, and squash. In autumn, they harvested nuts, berries, and rice. This was also a time for gathering herbs for medicines such as goldenseal and purple coneflower, which were used to treat colds. This seasonal life remained central to Ojibwes until into the twentieth century.

This historic photograph shows an Ojibwe woman at a sugar bush camp, cooking down the maple sap to make syrup and sugar.

FAMILY LIFE AND GOVERNMENT

CHAPTER 8

Ojibwes lived in family groups called **clans**. Clans were patrilineal, meaning children belonged to their father's clan. People could not marry within their own clan. Several clans lived together in a band. Bands came together for religious ceremonies, feasts, and social dances. Many bands make up the Ojibwe Nation.

Family values were strong among Ojibwes. Grandparents took part in raising children. White travelers often commented on Ojibwes' great affection for their children. "Even fathers are very kind to their sons," wrote one man. Children played with cornhusk dolls and ducks made out of cattails by relatives.

Ojibwe bands acted independently of one other. Each elected its own leader, the *ogimah*, and his advisers, called *anikeh-ogimauk*. Leaders were chosen by **consensus**, meaning the people all agreed on who the leaders would be. The people selected leaders who were considerate and wise.

This photograph shows the Ojibwe Chiefs Skinaway (left) and Wadena (with drum). In 1902, Wadena led a protest against the forced removal of the Ojibwes from the Mille Lacs Band Reservation to White Earth Reservation. Both men are shown wearing non-Ojibwe feathered headdresses.

When the U.S. and Canadian governments began treaty negotiations, Ojibwes found that whites expected to deal with a single tribal leader. They forced the Ojibwes to change their traditional government. Bands formed what became known as the Grand Council and elected a primary *ogimah*. The Grand Council was responsible for declaring war, negotiating peace, and developing laws.

BELIEFS

CHAPTER 9

Many Ojibwes believe in the Creator, who is neither male nor female. The Creator shares power with others—the trees, plants, animals, water, other spirits, and people—that are often messengers for the Creator, bringing the Midewiwin (a religious society of healers) dreams and spirit guides.

Dreams are an important part of Ojibwe religious beliefs. Boys and girls are encouraged to seek **visions**. During vision **quests**, Ojibwes receive dreams. They may also receive special lessons from an animal who becomes their spirit

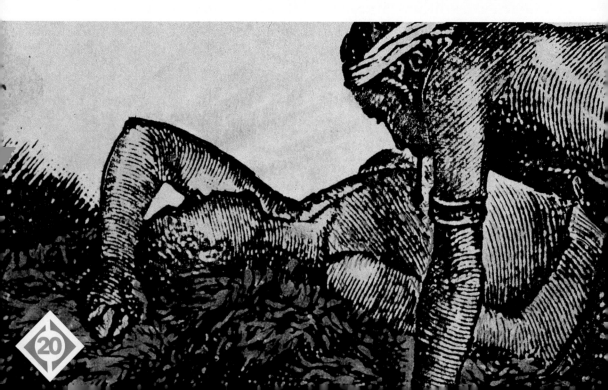

guide, or they may be shown how to use a medicine plant in a new way.

Depending on local traditions, there are four or eight levels of membership in the Midewiwin. Members are called Midé. They advance by completing lessons in proper behavior and in identifying and using medicines. They also learn how to read Midewiwin records written on birch-bark scrolls. Those at the highest levels know how to use rare herbs.

Among Ojibwes, native healers have traditionally been given the same respect as modern-day doctors because they can use herbs to treat sickness in people and bring them back to health. Becoming an Ojibwe healer takes a lifetime of education and practice.

Engraving of an Ojibwe healer, 1892

OJIBWE GOVERNMENT AND ECONOMY TODAY

CHAPTER 10

Today, about 120,000 Ojibwes live in Michigan, Wisconsin, Minnesota, and North Dakota in the United States and about 75,000 in Ontario, Manitoba, and Saskatchewan in Canada. They are the fourth-largest Native American group in the United States and the third-largest in Canada.

Each Ojibwe reservation in Canada elects its own *ogimah* and council. The reservations (called reserves in Canada) also send representatives to the Union of Ontario Indians (UOI). UOI works with the Canadian government, trying to ensure that the indigenous peoples receive proper health and educational programs.

In the United States, individual Ojibwe bands elect tribal councils consisting of a board with a chairperson. The Mille Lacs Band in Minnesota, however, has a governmental system similar to that of the United States.

The Ojibwe bands use the natural **resources** around them to provide employment. For example, in Wisconsin, the Red Cliff Band, the Bad River La Pointe Band, the Lac Courte Oreilles Band, and the Lac du Flambeau Band of Lake Superior Chippewa each own their own tribal hatchery to stock local rivers, lakes, and streams with fish. The Lac Courte Oreilles Band also owns a cranberry marsh at Chief Lake, a **hydroelectric** facility, and a lumber mill.

This welcome board to the Wikwemikong Reserve on Manitoulin Island in Canada proudly displays photos of some of its well-known residents, many of them celebrated artists.

CONTEMPORARY LIFE
CHAPTER 11

Ojibwe families who live on reservations today remain very close. Parents, children, grandparents, and other relatives get together often. They continue the tradition of hospitality and concern for their relatives

Traditional drumming plays a part in the weekly high school powwow on the Lac Courte Oreilles Reservation in Wisconsin.

and community. Ojibwes try to help each other and work for their communities to keep them strong.

On or off the reservation, Ojibwes live in the same types of houses as nonnatives. Ojibwes own TVs, radios, computers, video games, stoves, refrigerators, cars, and telephones. Like the rest of the world, bands are linked by high-speed Internet connections.

Children play ball in the yard, go to school, and do homework. Many speak three languages—English, French, and Ojibwe. Some take part in traditional ceremonies and have learned how to build birch-bark canoes, weave baskets, or bead clothing. They also help their relatives harvest wild rice and make maple sugar.

Many Ojibwes suffer from an illness called **diabetes**, which is often caused by eating unhealthy foods. Most bands tackle this problem by making people aware of what causes diabetes and encouraging them to eat more healthily.

Another widespread health problem is **addiction** to alcohol or drugs. The tribes are trying various ways to cure these addictions.

LITERATURE AND ART

CHAPTER 12

Artist Rebecca Belmore uses humor in her visual and performance art to help nonnatives see the often silly ways in which native people are depicted in popular culture. Her shows at the Canadian Museum of Civilization in Hull, Quebec, include "(I'm a) High-Tech Teepee Trauma Mama."

Sculptor Ron Noganosh also uses humor to get the meaning of his art across to people. Many of his works were created from items people have thrown away. In his sculpture *Will the Turtle Be Unbroken?* Planet Earth, dying from pollution, sits on a turtle shell that is carried through space on the starship *Enterprise*.

Louise Erdrich, the granddaughter of a tribal chief, has written both adult novels and children's books. In many of them, she describes about how the loss of land, children, and cultural traditions to whites' assimilation policies affect Ojibwe families. Her characters rely on humor and strong ties to traditions to get them through often harsh lives. *The Birchbark House, The Game of Silence,* and *The Porcupine Year* are a set of children's books Erdrich wrote about the lives of an Ojibwe girl and her family and tribe in the middle of the nineteenth century.

Ojibwe artist Rebecca Belmore

CURRENT ISSUES FACING THE OJIBWE

CHAPTER 13

In the 1980s, Ojibwes began taking the U.S. and Canadian governments to court over broken treaties. The Ojibwes proved in court that they had the right, as stated in the 1837 and 1850 treaties, to hunt and fish on the lands turned over to the U.S. and Canadian governments. The court agreed and said the Ojibwes could hunt and fish on what had been their lands at the time these treaties were signed.

This angered many nonnatives, who now claimed ownership of the land and who fished the waters. They claimed that the Ojibwes were threatening the supply of fish, but this was proven in court to be incorrect. Instead, it was **pollutants** from nonnative industries and nonnative sports anglers who had reduced fish populations.

The legal battles went all the way to the U.S. Supreme Court, which upheld the Ojibwes' rights to hunt and fish beyond the boundaries of the reservations. Today, white resort owners and sports anglers continue to **harass** Ojibwe fishermen despite court rulings.

Through this continued effort, and many other projects, the modern Ojibwes are successfully preserving their traditional lifestyles, language, and culture.

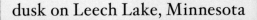

dusk on Leech Lake, Minnesota

GLOSSARY

addiction: The state of being unable to resist consuming certain substances, such as alcohol or drugs.

alliance: An agreement between two groups to work toward a common goal.

boarding school: A school that both teaches and houses children.

clan: A group of related families.

consensus: An agreement among all individuals in a group to an opinion or position.

council: A group of people who meet regularly to discuss issues or manage something.

culture: The arts, beliefs, and customs that form a people's way of life.

decoy: Something used to attract animals into a trap.

diabetes: A disease that causes problems with the body's ability to control the levels of sugar in the blood.

environment: The natural world.

harass: To put aggressive pressure on a person or persons.

hydroelectric: Having to do with the use of flowing water to generate electricity.

indigenous: Originating in a particular country or region.

negotiate: To discuss with others to come to an agreement.

pollutants: Substances that make air, water, or land dirty or impure.

quest: A journey to seek something.

reservation: Land set aside by the government for specific Native American tribes to live on.

resources: Materials available for use.

tan: To make into leather by soaking an animal skin in a special solution.

treaty: An agreement among nations or people.

visions: Things from the supernatural world that resemble dreams, only the person is awake.

FOR MORE INFORMATION

BOOKS

Sonneborn, Liz. *The Native American Experience.* Minneapolis, MN: Lerner Publishing, 2011.

Erdrich, Louise. *The Birchbark House.* New York, NY: Hyperion Books for Children, 2002.

Peacock, Thomas, and Marlene Wisuri. *The Good Path: Ojibwe Learning and Activity Book for Kids.* St. Paul, Minnesota: Minnesota Historical Society Press, 2009.

WEBSITES

Due to the changing nature of Internet links, PowerKids Press has developed an online list of websites related to the subject of this book. This site is updated regularly. Please use this link to access the list: www.powerkidslinks.com/sona/ojib

INDEX